Totem Beasts

Laurette Folk

ISBN: 978-1-945917-05-9

Printed in the United States of America

Front Cover Artwork: Laurette Folk
Back Cover Photo: Jurek Schreiner
Cover Design: Christopher Reilley

Also by Laurette Folk:

A Portal to Vibrancy

BIG TABLE Publishing

"Making other books jealous since 2004"

Big Table Publishing Company
Boston, MA
www.bigtablepublishing.com

Acknowledgements

Many thanks to Jennifer Colella Martelli for her honest critique and belief in this book; thank you to Jennifer Jean, Kim Aubrey, Olivia Kate Cerrone, and Andrea Tupper for reading, critiquing, and cheering me on; thank you to Denise Koelsch for her compassion and lessons in Shamanism; thank you to Robin Stratton for being flexible and diligent; and a hearty thanks to the following publications that first featured some of the poems and flash fiction published here:

Literary Mama: "The Child Behind the Wall," "Zygotes, Hatched and Delivered"
Italian Americana: "My Grandfather, the Christ," "Dud"
805 Lit + Art: "Death"
The Mom Egg Review: "Suspended in Holy Alluvium," "Retreat"
Chicago Literati: "The Last Dauphin," "Therapy Dog, "A Gathering of Women"

For my family

Table of Contents

I. Stasis

Totem Beasts

There are no ghosts in this house.
        No hem of a muslin dress
draped over a riser.
        No Emily Dickinson archetype
figured prominently at the banister.
        No face in the naked glass.

The boreal firs, always a regiment,
        are noble, melancholic as the
tide bathes the sedge.

We listen for what the hayfield says.
                We wait
for totem beasts, but no coyote parts these
        fallow fields. No moose. No
osprey in wake of wind.
        Quotidian, these crows, those gulls.

I am filled with pale green air.
        My sister's child thumps in Utero.
Clouds snuff the sun, the sacrament, the
        fiery heart.

Night comes.

I sit quietly inside myself.
        My father bows his head here,
the lines echoing around his eyes.

The Slow Pale Rise of Indigo

The slow pale rise of indigo taps
  at the door of the Underworld—
it wants to walk here, free.

It knows
every twilight is a prophecy
  and the visible carries
the invisible on its back.

Our last breath passes through tarnished
  skin and
clogs the holes in our bones.
  We fret, catch the slack vowels
of the lullabies we sing ourselves.

Something stands between me and the
  morning glory's cup of prayer.
Its thin vine grasps at every near thing.
  At night, it wrings itself tightly
as if it had hands.

The Child Behind the Wall

So let's tell it straight.
They send him into a room
to do his thing
grab his weight in cash.
I've got my legs spread
for a gelled dildo and plastic
umbilical cords.
The monitor displays screens
of pixelated shadows.

Optimistic folk
tell me about a 45 first
the blessing of twins
and Baby Jay
but their stories are as stale
as a decade's crumbs.

They told me you would come
two years ago now.
An herbalist's tricks might
prod this old fruit.
But I've drawn no door
in the wall through which
to call you home.

Colmar, France

My net is extended to catch exotic
ascending words in the streets
of Colmar, France.

I take them back to my room
examine their wings, let them fly
around. My breath quickens.
My tendons tighten. The words land
on lampshades, the rim of the showerhead.
They coagulate in the curtains.

You are a waiter in a cafe wearing
a black vest and cowboy boots
with a collection of words for auction.

We barter.

Your words sing, snap, flutter
in the ether. I fumble with my net. You
sniff at my offerings. Keep some.
Toss others.

Sitting in your corner of the world,
I am shaded from the hard sun.
Your roses droop with faces
of wine and lace. The grapes
in the hills above us claim the nutrients
of the Earth.

My words become food. Your words
become cash. Cash becomes time.

All passes.

Intimacy

I am intimate with the hot bullet
that strikes the deer's heart and tears
it in two.

I know the moment
he unzips his flesh and it
falls to the ground, freeing up
the deer soul inside.

I am intimate with the hare's
perpetual fear of being eaten.

With the hawk's talons
that clutch the soft fur, strangling
the fear into nothing.

I am intimate with the soul child
stolen from the flesh
of her mother's womb.

With the hole in a beggar's bowl.

Who tears the curtain in the temple?
Who pummels the nails into Christ's palms?

I lift the sponge to his tongue.

Communion

The cumulous clouds   are pregnant with vapor
There is a rocket of light to the east.
What static electrifies this lonely body?
Still it does not rain, no

The trees show the backs of their hands,
The birds are silenced between limbs.
I go to church, sit near the door for easy escape
I don't belong there in a red dress
I don't belong there with neither a coin
nor a blessing.

Your falling star burned to nothing
before it reached me—
the harbinger—
who seeks communion and a catch basin—

for all that is rushing.

Another Egg to Crack

The mind, my mind, is a petulant child
always touching things it shouldn't
making a big stink in its pants. Just
sit down. No, that's not for you. Here
look at this. Play with this for a while.

Every day my life is an egg to crack.
Inside, the yolk has spoiled, so I,
the small bird that I am, peck at the
shell. Peck, peck, peck. I create
a hole, stick out a drenched wing
roll out an eye.

Other people don't think of shells
or spoiled yolks. They think of money.

I dreamt last night my father
was a criminal. The police
landed on the roof in a gray copter.
When they took down the door, my
father went willingly.

I faced him on the other side
of bullet proof glass
So this is where you've been?
A man like you?

I wake and my father is still dead.
The squirrels are stuffing
their cheeks with nature's offerings.
It is another day.
Another child to pull by the hand.

Another egg to crack.

Devotion is a Patient Landscape

The land lies tilled and ready.

We rove over highways and I count
raptors. Mr. Eight perches majestically
eyeing dinner. We slow for tolls
groan with every braking. You
squeeze my knee.

The clouds unfurl their curtains,
the backdrop for weeping blossoms.
Spring has come to Pennsylvania.

I gaze into a compact mirror at
white hairs and blemishes. Imperfect.

Indeed it has been a long vacant
New England winter
but now I must speak of
our unspoken devotion.

We wander the cemetery on the hill
separate, search for the epitaphs of your
ancestors interred in German sepulchers.

I spot you attempting to decipher
the illegible.

I may have my imaginative musings.
In my mind I am a vagrant.
Perhaps you are too.

I travel away from you
visit foreign countries of thought.

You do too.

But devotion is a fallow field
a patient landscape.
In this burgeoning world
among the dead
there you are.

Fresh Eyes

I've spent the evening crumpled
on the couch and come to bed
early morning, see the lump
of blankets that is you.

We toss, restless.
The sheet becomes untucked.
The radiator hisses and clangs.

In the morning, your face.
Your man eyes have a thousand
endearing facets.
I rest my head on your chest.

Marriage is a box.
We throw ourselves
up against the walls.
Writhe.
Get out of bed.

You tell me I could use
some mystique.
You begrudgingly
see the transformation
how I get dressed
spray perfume
become my outside self.

Your confession is this
you want to see me
as other men see me.
With fresh eyes.

Something in my body
is ignited by your words.

I will keep them with me
in that box inside myself,
a gift I unwrap
throughout the day.

Amanda

We were traveling along the interstate somewhere near Boston and we stopped when we saw them—people, children crawling over the infrastructure like rats. We too decided to do this, hang from the beams, shimmy ourselves between gusset plates, swing like monkeys from the girders. Before long, we all huddled in a corner near the south wingwall and regarded the piles of children's clothes in the street—socks and underwear mainly. Others were still up there swinging, and it became a show of sorts. At one point a limo pulled up. We stood starstruck as beautiful actresses in long gowns walked into the street. My father had written to one of them (perhaps it was Kim Bassinger) and he signed his name Amanda. He was always signing his name Amanda after the seizures, my mother said.

Longing

My brother and I were waiting in the basement of the healer's house in the vestibule annexed to the sanctuary when we got stuck. I had longed for this private sacristy—the singing bowl, burning sage, and prayer to the four directions—and took a chance coming to her this late in the evening. When she did not show up, I surmised she was depleted and needed respite. Even healers need to sleep.

The door had curiously locked behind us, so we wandered the catacombs of her basement, passing through several portals until we found ourselves at the dark belly of the furnace. We debated what to do; they would think we were stealing if we made ourselves known. So I dipped the baby in the commode and made the sign of the cross on her brow. Then we lingered anxiously behind a door left ajar and spied on the healer's husband in his easy chair as he watched television, his Bob Ross hair flying off his head, his feet up. At some point we heard the husband's soft snoring. When we had conjured up enough courage, we tried a door next to the television; it led to a stairway and out to the front hall. Here we opened a second door into the night.

In a leafless tree, an owl spread his wings. He was white with brown specs on his breast and had yellow eyes that looked down into one's own nakedness. He was fierce but elegant, and his wings took up most of the star-speckled southern sky. We stepped out, free, and he flew up into the night, his giant head adjusting like the moon.

Magdalene, Betrayed

I rushed down the steps of the museum
late for my rendezvous with a Jewish friend
who had been texting me secrets
in a dead language.

Colonnades presented angularity
stiff and inexorable: a firm, obstinate grasp
on reality; steps, avenues, buildings lay
between us, obstacles to be overcome
in time and space.

Dark cloaks were hung on the walls of the city
and worn in the streets. I passed the revered senile
priest escorted by his mistress. He was dressed
in wet gauze and his phallus was engorged,
visible under the clinging veil.

I recall now, how, at a table in the round
I mentioned the Buddha's name
and private heads nodded.
I recall how I rushed down that flight of stairs
of the medieval museum
without thinking of the forsaken
Magdalene in cadmium red.

I'll tell you what that kiss on the mouth
meant. It meant choice, like Judas's kiss
meant choice, but his was betrayal.

Christ had something else in mind.

The Beasts

I watch through a glass door and see my father walk by with Sasquatch behind him. Sasquatch stops, looks directly at me, but my father continues on, leaving the frame. Later the beast returns and I learn that it's a she. She's lost much of her hair; she's even wearing clothes, accessories, a t-shirt and shorts, a pearl necklace and earrings. I open the sliding glass door and let her in. When she steps inside, I see just how tall she is—her head nearly touches the ceiling of the Great Room. Where do you live? I ask her. How do you survive? She says her kind comes out just before dawn. There is a community that rises early purposely to cater to them. They feed them, bathe them, cut their hair. It is, the she-yetty says, a clandestine operation.

So I think about this, about what happens below the radar of the media, how this compassion between species isn't reported, primarily because it would be usurped by something else, but I'm unsure what this something else is.

Others from her tribe come; they have the countenances of trolls: big ears and noses, ruddy cheeks, hair inconsistently spread throughout their bodies. For a moment we all look at one another and regard our physical differences, the Sasquatches and myself, the Sasquatches and my family, who remain fairly demure throughout all this, and I know not how they truly feel about being a part of this underground railroad. We all stand in the air of the Great Room with the portraits of our imperious, discerning ancestors around us, waiting, but still my father does not come, is doing something else, some important thing that will keep us all safe.

Access Denied

It's a fine day in March for snowshoeing
and we take the new path abutting the CSA farm
where there is now a fence—the same fence
at which the deer halt and peer in
at all that is ripe and lush.

Uphill, I trudge, the claws of my snowshoe
scratch at old ice as I search for the portal
they had found through the brambles.
I loosen my scarf and unzip my coat,
useless, a heavy hide across my shoulders.

The slender trunks of gray rise up
from mottled white and scrape the blue sky;
my dog trots her lady dog trot beside me.
My sister, behind me, is further away now
thinking of all the things she could be doing.

I saw them early one fall morning
in the pink mesh of the thicket
crossing the creek, a heard of quiet
in the woods, surefooted and sentient.
They startled me, and I them
and they went to higher ground through
this portal in the brambles.

They perched above me, silent
as if they were etchings on a cave wall
A flutter of tails, mythical creatures.
They vanished.

This way, I shout to my sister
who has turned back, who has lost hope
who has no time for guesswork.

My dog nervously pants, as a slender
green whip catches my thigh and
another scratches my cheek. A fallen
limb here, there, my snowshoe a shutter
swaying on its hinge. I lose my pole and it
too is a slender thing in the snow.

I fight. I slash at the thorns,
I stab and curse all of the year's failures.
Like a tall oak, I sway and creak.
A tendril claws at my cheek.

In the snow—prints, pellets;
They could be watching.
I stare at the woods, waiting for it
to configure an entrance.
I think of coming through.

I want to come through.

My sister's voice is small
and importunate
and I give up, eventually.
Head back to the farm
where I'm supposed to be
where the path is wide and easy.

Gardener's Poem

Lust begets a feverish mind
switching from this to that to this
configuring beauty with blossom
or the lack thereof.

Quick, knock out those lethal specks
on the zucchini flowers
buds collapsing on themselves,
delicate yellow laundry
wrung by invisible hands.

Pull the lettuce forming a stalk.
Crack it open
and it bleeds a bitter milk
A bitter lie to the tongue.

Quick, dig up the diminutive rose
aside the blind peony;
caress every unearthed root.
Replace the corner rose
whose only bloom is a ray
once the solstice turns.

Defy the image in your mind—a banquet.
Come to terms with how it is:
just like everything else—
a thing trying to get by.

Acknowledge the need for grace
from the god
who delegates 1000 angels to one body

who at any one moment can exalt himself
above the banal,
but chooses not to
most of the time.

Death

Blood retreats to the four corners.
The mind says to the heart: you're
Fired. Get your shit and get out.
The heart telephones the soul
Listen, there's a train leaving
In an hour. The soul,
That quicksilver flash—

In the late summer
When the flowers turn to seed
And the birds fall from the sky to
Rampage the stalks,
Death counts his money. His skin
Is draped over his bones like an
Oiled hide, his limbs felled.

The grass parts and a throng arrives
In black hats and bonnets. They unravel bills
From their fists and Death pours
A round for everyone.
Through the fields they go,
Young again.

Above them, wings.

I recall now, how it was—
The six-legged angels
Tapping at the windows.
The stone rolled away from our
Front door.

The sheets cast aside.

In this cleared space
He speaks a word
Well below my audible range.

It is something in the air, rarefied.
I collect it in the cells of my lungs,
Push it
        through the ventricles
           of my
                Heart.

My Grandfather, the Christ

They carried you out on a stretcher
swathed in white.
Your daughter saw in your face
a suffering Christ.

Your wife bathed you, fed you broth,
put a warm cloth to your temples.

Your prodigal son shaved your beard
and confessed his sins.

You took Sunday sojourns to the Sound,
You had your share of 40 days and 40 nights.
You spun our small world like Atlas
while we giggled and scrambled
away from your outstretched arms.

You once exclaimed you were a small man
who used small words.

But when you died

you took the word in my hand
multiplied it one hundred fold
and filled the room with a new language

we must now learn to speak.

Icon, Idol, Model Man

You are a place in my mind
and I am a person
You, icon, idol, model man,
tresses on your shoulder
long and lithe when you
stand and rock the boat
bare thigh, a flash.
We lay on a raft
made of saplings and drift
toward a shipwreck in
Gloucester Harbor where
there are night swimmers
and other incorporeal beings.
You, too, are a ghost
and yet your hand is pure
sensation
You take down my shirt
and expose my skin
to the stars.

Later, you break me
and I break you, entomb
you in a mountain cave
like Antigone.

When the evening wanes
and the dishes are put away
and the children asleep
I return to you, my private
lust, my evensong.

The Madonna at the Table

We have come round this table for a feast
harboring your secret.

We pass the potatoes, pour wine.
We have spoken of war, of soldiers
drafted by fate, ravaged not by bullets
but deviant cells.

Lauretta Philomena, we watched your bones
the exacting shape of your skull in kerchiefs.
We accompanied you to witch doctors
adorned your head with other people's
hair. Listened as you spoke with your
eyes. Of terror. Regret. The end of love.

Peter Angelo, we found your MRIs
in a manila folder in the trash.
Technicolor maps depicting the
countries of tumor, brain, eyeball
pummeled with the remnants
of rotting meat scraps, broccoli stalks
and old bills.

We witnessed your spirit fly out
leave the front door wide open.
When they came to take your body
we ran and hid.

Ferdinand Cipriano, we knelt at your
bedside. We lay our hands on you,
soaked the sweat from your forehead
with cool cloths.

Did you imagine the confluence of
good and evil? Ponder how to cleave
this place with a blade, free yourself?

You were the first to lie to us.

Loretta R., you died not knowing
your own name. We asked one
another, What landscape is this?
Who stole the script?

Did the dead coax you thither?
A deity distract you
with lies? Sometimes you smiled
at the lurk and leisure of the nameless
but your open eyes were closed shades.
Through you we had come to know
the Landscape of the Erased.

The sick have long been buried.
We have spent years weeping lost
in the underworlds of grief. We
have seen the spark of inchoate life
dim and die. We have known the
arrest of the infertile.

You, sister, are our Madonna
in a borrowed periwinkle sweater.
We shall sit with you, break bread, wait
for life. Tender, vibrant, rapacious life.

Stone Devil

We are at my grandmother's bedroom perusing her relics—crosses, beads, jewels. My childhood friend exclaims there is a devil behind the closet door. There is a party downstairs as well, company from the 1970s. The doorbell is continuously ringing. The devil knocks, wants to come out. There is laughter and shouting. Some joker is serving deviled eggs. My grandmother is long gone from this room, but if we venture downstairs to the den, we might find her in a flowery dress, her hair done up in fat curls, an Elizabeth Taylor smile across her lips. My childhood friend tells me I should answer the door. It takes my opening the door to turn the devil to stone; he resides in my hands now, a small orange relic with wings, something that can be broken.

I descend down to the den with the devil tucked under my arm. I enter different Polaroid snapshots of relatives in bell bottom jeans and rock band belt buckles, smoothed rumps, cat-eye glasses, elegant fingers pivoting cigarettes, tanned leather, and scotch for the men. People are smiling; they have no idea what awaits them in the future. I mingle. I shiver. I fret. People are laughing and smoking; smoke veils the room. I don't belong here, in the past where life is cool and easy. No one here is serious. No one here knows just how serious life can be.

The Shack at Land's End

The shack at Land's End was my mother's and I was a visitor there. It was a small gray weather-beaten shack with white trim. The sparse lawn led down to the rocks where the waves split open white. The night I was there, a storm was coming and there were thirty footers crashing offshore. My mother was excited by the storm; she said the dark clouds, the lightning, the looming waves exhilarated her. I, on the other hand, was somewhat apprehensive: they were airlifting full-suited businessmen paralyzed with fright from the surf (yachts and other small crafts were capsizing left and right). An emergency tanker the size of a small city was flickering off shore. Upstairs, in a loft, there was a pillow in the shape of the world. I retreated there to punch it flat and make it stay. Then I rode the world down the stairs as if it were a sled. The storm broke. Pieces of dark sky floated hither and thither—celestial flotsam and jetsam. The impending storm wouldn't be what we thought, and we would have to go on with our dull, worrisome lives.

II. Swollen Mandala

Suspended in Holy Alluvium

We coo, my sister and I.
    Spy a sleeper in a vault
of shadows

a pipefish
    suspended in holy alluvium.

Oh God, there. Look:
    the delicate linking of bone
Now supine, now suckling.

I have lain here myself
    with tickets of eggs to be torn.

I have catered to stasis
    as a touchstone caters to the blind.

Have learned the tenets
    of a hollow woman's creed. But

now I am dazzled by form.

We revel in this code that builds.
We revel in the alphabet of our cells

writ by mystery's hand.

I Dive In

My grandmother blooms
above the thorns in my hair, nightly.
She smiles her perfect teeth smile
meanders around the room,
picks up a spoon, a wine glass.
Her ebony hair
a memory, her diaphanous silk
gown, a figment.

The dead are shy. Speak at six
decibels below our audible range.
We can touch only what they leave
behind—the spoon, the wineglass.

Here is the table in the dining room
hunks of aged parmesan cheese, sliced
pepperoni and roasted red peppers
sour artichoke hearts, salami you
roll with the tongue.

Permanent stains of oil and wine.

We sit at the table and tell our stories
We point, the Messiah is the one in red
with opened arms. The others
all hands. There is a skull
in the sink, its watchful eyes.

Here is the light that falls
across my grandmother's linoleum
floor, its gold seams and screws
illumed.

There is the bridge. All the water
I own in fecundity flows beneath me.
The state of the child, to the right.
The state of the childless to the left.

I dive in.

Zygotes, Hatched and Delivered

They show us a portrait
of four mystic cells.
In a sterile room,
I am the showcase,
the Diva in blue.

But we're all blue
with blue pants and
blue shirts and blue
shower caps—
antiseptic, joyless creatures.

You sit there harboring regrets
as a man's gloved hands shake
between my thighs.
I squirm and bite, taste
sharp, metallic edges.

Count pressures
in hidden places.

A boy-faced man mutters
fine, fine...
I grab your hand,
the only skin on skin
in the room.

I am lukewarm water and wood
a taut wire of entrails
between skyscrapers.
I am a reservoir
swallowing trees,

a deluge on a forgotten town.

Then we see them.
Pixels on the screen.
A flash of ethereal white.

Science bursts.
Perfect, someone says.
Perfect.

Swollen Mandala

Everything white, as if baked in a kiln.
Moon hazed now, my one hundred year old
eyes closing, a song hidden just under my skin
demands an ear or two. The seeds
have been sewn. The sacred chant and
four rosettes are embedded in the
swollen mandala. I summon the myths
of my ancestors, the mountains supine
and shadowless, the labyrinth on the hill,
the chapel, the Golgotha of cacti crosses.
Huddled in the back pews, the Indigenous
their dark eyes, pious heads. I walked
the labyrinth to settle my nerves while
their sorrows protruded through the dirt
like small weeds.

My sister's child is a molded angel
white as the dust in that kiln. There
on the sill, stone wings draped in leaves.
Take root, I say to the rosettes, unfolding.
Lay your pious heads on the translucent pillow,
wrap yourselves in the crimson sheets
and be lulled by song.

Three Blind Moles Attach

Three blind moles attach
to my uterus, their luminescent
heads subtly bob, their bodies
curl and tuck. My silent world
closes on their soft round skulls.
Help. This is the word
choked out, then swallowed. Help.
The sedum, ubiquitous in September,
is pink with nausea, the crab apple tree
has forgotten its fruit, the sky,
wrapped in Lazarus's shrouds, holds
out both arms to Mother Earth
who thrusts open her legs. I retract
from their lovemaking.

Slumber is as thick as weeds.

The small pat, the unleavened bread,
rises in each blind mole,
a tap tap tap telegraph to souls
whose wings darken rooftops

and valleys.

I lay this body down,
toss out statistics
and pitch the head of Science
on a stick—a notable totem
for an autumn night.

In the Garden of Limbo

In the garden, sleek, semi-clothed women
reach up their slender arms like ribbons
to be taken by the wind. I spy an exotic bloom,
wispy, pink, almost colorless, like a creature,
ethereal and weightless, at the bottom
of the sea. I gurgle and pop, spoil, blip, blip...
The fishes, now in gill and fin stage, flip,
like a catch on the deck. I want to unzip myself
and set them free in the fountain with one lotus
and its high-stalked perch for a damselfly
or a dew drop or a wandering spore.
These fishes will swim through stars and holes,
rise, like sacred bread; I am sustenance
for their hungry mouths. When they split me open,
and untangle their cords, I will know their holy,
untouchable lives. And only then will I know love.

Diaphanous Moments

This morning my uterus
coughed up a dustball,
the discarded claws and dander
of the rabbits burrowing silently
in the soil of my womb.
I place myself inside myself
and witness the slow crawl of atoms
of silence and sinew and sweet-meat.
I spy, float between you,
tethered by thought strings.
See there, a twitch, a solitary stimuli,
the trajectory of a comet aside
vacant ovary moons and a whirling
saturnine bowel with probing eye.

I open my eyes
and the solar system shrinks.
There is a dark cave to my stomach;
out belches dust, the murmurs
of the supine and sleeping hares.
They feed. They dance.
I am chained to this incubator,
to these belching caves.
I pray for the blessing of the fleet.
People tell you all sort of things.
Secrets. Lies. They hoard
the glistening pennies in the well.
They say nothing.
I wait for those diaphanous moments,
those gems when I see
my child hand in God's hand,
my child's hand in my hand.

To Eat an Egg

I must go eat an egg
to stave off the hellions.
The days pop up like worms
in the rain. They inch along
blackened streets; I am careful
not to crush each delicate flesh.

The one who removes the necklace
of dew off the morning grass
has been long forgotten. I am
more content with a leafless tree
or nearly leafless, with a smattering
of gold or vermillion, the memory
of Earth fire rising in gray ash.

In the last of the green grass,
my father, in a black and red
barn coat, raises an ax over a log.
His breath is released from his lips
into the gray air. I look back
at him now, his speckled beard,
his half-worn hat, and reach for him
through an opened sash
but feel only his vapor
on my outstretched arms.

I must eat that egg.
I must rest and soothe
the currents driving the tides

of this body, this vessel of
water, bone, and blood for those
who will be named,
who will be clay
for his invisible hands.

Subtle Branding

Summer's wealth manifests itself
in the last of the leaves as my beating heart
pushes blood to their hungry bellies.
The aurora behind my eyes darkens.
The cave straight down the middle of me
echoes their grunts.

My husband chops wood
out in the yard as my father used to do.
Sometimes I confuse the two.
Dad, I want to call down to the cellar,
Dad? Dad?

Now here is Philomena
a floral house dress hiding her girth,
walking the path behind the woodpile.
I have known the inside of her home,
the smell of camphor and gas,
the rumble of her cauldron of sauce,
the braised letters of the old language
flavoring her telling of tales

to her aging children
who, in turn, told each other stories
of infidelity, gambling, and bastards.

These are my people
sitting at the table
with tiny silver goblets
of Sambuca, the air redolent of cigarette ash
and some Neapolitan crooner:
tutto e bene quel che finisce bene, they say.

Behind the woodpile, I take
Philomena's hand.
I am the great granddaughter,
the *Medigan*, who wants to show
the old mother my world.

Philomena, with her stockings rolled
down to her ankles, her soft leather shoes
molded to her bunions, is afraid.
Of what I know not. Wild dogs?
Gypsies? These are of the old country.
But conquering one new world
is enough for her.

In the silence of the late autumn light,
I turn her around. She holds firmly
to my arm and we both mute, carefully,
make our way home.

It is evening and slender limbs
trace their names in the sky.
My husband has stacked the wood.
My children nap down in that cave
among the stories scratched into the wall.
The light of the fire blazes,
a subtle and gentle branding of each letter
into the backs of their skulls.

The Klein House

Above the valley where the little Lehigh flows,
the Klein house, built of gray river stone
tops a green knoll and has its eyes on the river.
Years ago, when the settlers lived,
they figured amongst that small river life
dug for crayfish in the fertile banks or
doused cloth in the water like a preacher
his penitents, the draped trees with their soft
tresses at their backs, the brambles at the banks
with tart berries swallowed whole by lovers
with its wine-like juice on their tongues.

Imagine now, flour in the creases of the palms
of the eldest girl, the moist rise of bread
inside the hearthstone with her thoughts
baked inside, a woman's rising stitch
that extends the life of the cloth, a man's
yielding bones in the fields, the sinew of
his muscle, toiling with earth, coaxing it.

Imagine also a boy's hands, tugging
at the ruddy knobs of udders, the toll
of the bell in the fields beckoning the beasts
return, the formidable toll of a higher bell
on Sundays where a log cabin chapel
houses their pious heads bowed
in the direction of the pews as the river
flows high or low, a constant murmuring
under joined voices, a source of water
for their daily ablutions.

We ramble among their graves, elevated
among the bones that once knew motion
that once knew the same code of blood
now pulsing through the nascent forms
inside my womb, that code of what you
will be, diggers by a different river,
lovers with wine-like juice on your tongues.

Love Delivers

Love delivered the estranged
to my doorstep,
the cherubs who curl and yawn
an inch above my groin.

Love delivered the saint, the mystic
the artist, the imagination
that illuminates the page,

the expanse of fern over bedrock,
you, taciturn and gentle. Wise.

Love delivered this hump,
that hump;

It gathers its wits now
crosses its t's and dots its i's
while he sleeps and she awaits
his face, this cool bud
growing toward her window.

III. Lessons in Subtlety

Whispers

There has been the smashing of boats
I find their pieces—tassels of wet rope
A shard of hull
A blade.

A bird without a name perches
Unafraid of propinquity
Light filters through a closed portal
Like God.

The subtlety of health
Has to do with what you tell yourself
And how you abandon the myths of anxiety
Those ghosts you must keep in the corner
Of your eye.

Above all, remember this:
Suffering is interesting
And there is no drug
That will teach you patience

So let them comb your hair
Whisper in your ear and ease
The stiffness in your spine
And you will fall asleep
Under a shade tree
Dreaming of rest.

Est Deus in Nobis

What are you reaching for?

What are you yearning for?

You, craving this beauty
or that truth
stirring like the vixen at two
in the morning, her haunt wailing
under a hollowed out moon.

I opened the door
and cold early May stepped inside
while two stars sat like birds
on the horizon.

I went back to sleep.

In a dream, I walked to a shrine
in the woods where men
were learning to genuflect
and women ceremoniously disrobed
displaying each middle-aged body
each forgotten hip and lacy breast.

In a vestibule, Asian scholars
translated texts recently unearthed,
young people with wide brows
reached out their hands to me.

I went to the door

and worried I would not get back in.
Outside the shrine, beyond
the wing-backed stones
beyond the fat, loose vines
and rusted gate were artists
peddling their wares.

I wanted to stop. I could have stopped,

but this wayward beggar of thoughts—
yours, his, hers—this wayward beggar
of thoughts that I am,
I rambled on.

The Circe's Cabin

The duke and I stumbled upon her cottage in the woods with the front door open. We went in, delighted by the cozy living quarters decorated with colorful textiles and marble statues, Buddha stones, shrines of goddesses, stained glass, and damask curtains. We settled on a duvet on the floor and the duke, with his multi-colored eyes and ebony hair, read from Sappho's lost book of poems. The poems were printed on papyrus and turned to dust in his hands, but with every new page we marveled at the secret words until the sun set and the lights began to flicker across the bay.

Afterward, we went out to the deck; half of it was falling into the water, its wood curved like a cascading wave. There were others now, figured on neighboring decks, gossiping, raising their glasses, seemingly content as the water lapped at the banks. Inside, more people had arrived and sat on the couch with drinks in their hands. Dogs were chasing each other around the fireplace. Lovers were eating muffins in the breakfast nook dropping crumbs on the floor. Then she arrived. She was not ageless. She was not beautiful. She was surprised to see us all there, taking advantage of her lair. I told her I would make it right. I frantically went about collecting the dust, hair, and shards of glass in my hands. What was she to do now? The place was a sty and the lord and his mistress were renting it for a getaway. I looked after the duke but he had disappeared. I told the others to get out. A man fell from the roof and broke his neck. Another was eating an orchid on the front porch.

When I last saw the duke, he was arm in arm with the crone as she lead him into her bedroom and then locked the door. Not an hour later, she released him to the paddock where he rummaged for scraps, squealing and snorting his way through the sounder of swine.

They arrived and I had the place spotless and vacant, save the crone who hummed softly as she braided her hair in her chamber. The man with the broken neck had been airlifted to the nearest hospital. The lights across the bay had gone out. The pigs had stuffed themselves silly. I opened the door and they were young and dark: the lord wore an oversized baseball cap and a medallion, the mistress, sweatpants with LOVE printed across her ass. They talked to each other as if I didn't matter, commenting on the place, delighted to be there, and alone.

To the Underworld and Back, a Poem

There is a schism in a cliff in Maine
Where I slipped down through the moss
And knelt in the sand of the river bank

A gilded snake coiled my head, a crown
A carried cloak muffled my ears
Then turned to wings.

I flew above the firs, I flew
Knowing how to fly, I flew.

I dove, knowing how to dive
And emerged among the women
Lounging without a care on rocks

Picking at Damariscotta oysters
Licking salted pearls, humming
And pruning till nightfall.

At the shore, my father's form flickered
As the morning fog dusted the cove
He was horse. He was man.

He was horse again.

I grabbed his mane and hoisted myself
Upon his back and rode out
Remembering, how he carried me

(When I was far too old for carrying).

Encounters

They toppled trees, cleared paths to open
the woods and flush out the homeless vets
pitching tents, sleeping in the oak leaves.

I saw the two moon tracks first—incredulous,
that my neighborhood's patch of woods
could support something as big as deer.

She came to eat the tops of fallen trees.
We came to walk the new paths and view
the river from a different perspective,
climb the rungs of roots, and run loose.

Across the river, skaters motored and
scraped their boards at dusk. Through the
box elders you can see the light turn red.

Across the river, the nameless guard
their personal space, hunched over,
waiting for the train to let down her steps.

I only see her when I am not looking
when I am head-down walking
and then a flash of white, a flash of wing
from another world.

A Treacherous Environment

Someone said there was a river of acid running through the land. A navy seal had already died trying to traverse it; his body turned to stone. The thing about foreign, treacherous environments is that you best keep your wits about you or you're dead. If you expose your skin to the air above the river, it would seize up and fall off. This was the warning. I moved into the river of acid and had it take me. It rocked a cavern between shafts of pleasing orange light. I saw the body of stone.

(Look at the sky, my great uncle said. Look at your blessed grandmother's face. Behold everything, a fine bottle of wine, a cupped hand at the table. He lives in a houseboat now and no longer knows his children's names; he drifts with the current of the river and is content with where it takes him.)

I turned with the river until it spit me out. They told me it was poison, but I didn't feel a thing.

The Ohio River Valley

I was returning home from college with my packed bags and was changing trains when I met an old friend in the station. Or perhaps we were traveling together. Or perhaps she was a ghost and only I could see her. She may have communicated to me something about a mutual friend accomplishing an unidentified goal. The ghost friend was excited about our mutual friend accomplishing this goal. Perhaps she was on her way to see her. Perhaps not. She got off the train once we reached the station, and I continued with my journey home to Wakefield where my parents lived. I remember quite clearly asking the conductor if I was on the right train. He said I was. The train disembarked and took wide turns through the country where we passed lush meadows of green watercress or maybe alfalfa, a barn with a trellis of zucchini so large they looked like zeppelins ready to split at the seams. Soon we had passed Wakefield and were headed for the Ohio River Valley. "I've never been to Ohio," I said to myself, excited about a new land. At dusk, we reached the river where they were gathered at the embankment, my parents and their contemporaries, listening for the animal sounds echoing in the silhouetted mountains and across the mists of the river. Coyote cry, wolf howl, hawk screech, elk—all calling out to the incoming darkness.

Things with Wings

An angel with dirty feet grabs ahold
To something in that tree

His filigree wings beat at the air
He is more faint than fair

A distant cousin, perhaps, to Marquez's
Old man with Enormous Wings

Whom they put in a cage

And sold tickets to the pious
To gawk at and the sinners to tease.

I'm sure if I had a ladder I could climb
To him and look into his yellow

Eye and know that such angels
Have the same aches and pains

As I, the only thing separating us
Would be a height of twelve feet or more.

Lo, his wings open full on, and I swear
The world went dark for a moment,

As he fluttered, fumbled, up, up. He knew
(They all know) when you're just too close.

Back on the north side of Green Hill,
The egrets pruned and waited for the tide

To unfold in fish, the grand dame,
A river herself in curves and elegance,

Bent toward the water as if to say
What have we here? I watched the lesser

Egrets do nothing as the breeze
Excused itself from the trees and I paused

And bowed my head,
I bowed my head, yes.

Undisturbed

I go to Alewife Station
past the boarded up dance clubs, across
the forgotten marsh, past the
low income housing rising up,
a brick totem toward the sky.

I once met a friend here
drank orange juice in her junked
Saab, while the gulls chased
balled-up trash—tumbleweeds
across the heaves in the parking lot.

Now, I am with you, tending
the fire under the church in Sedona,
Black dogs are here, one male—he licked
your fingers as you lay dying,

the other, female, her ear a flag
off her head—my current familiar.

We sit between them.

I forced down a McMuffin after
the juice just as the
the electric summer morning sun sent
me reeling before we headed North.

I was disappointed by my inability
to be, well, normal, as I often perceived
normal in others. That is un-disturbed.

I want to tell you I have learned to see.
I have learned to see the cool cattails
bend in the wind beneath
the infrastructure.

I have learned to see the marsh, there,
through the traffic, through the broken
fenders, and shattered glass.

Just as I have always been there,
here, cool beneath these nerves.

Retreat

She came in the guise of my dog to lure me away, as Apollo lured Achilles away from the walls of Troy. I saw her from the window running through the marsh and had a choice to make, to follow her, or stay and do what others expected me to do—listen attentively to the poet reading, stay near my children who were being watched by respectable God-fearing teenagers in the next room. I opted to go (not that I chose her over them, but to me her name spelled f-r-e-e-d-o-m), follow her over a plank bridge through the mud flats where red wings sang out in raspy trills and swayed precariously on cattails. She kept running, taking me farther away, over the sloping fields and into an old farmhouse where she disappeared up a staircase that ended at a window. Vanished. I was left alone on the stairway and then was not alone; people brought in cold sesame noodles and Jell-o molds, set them on a long white-clothed table below, and went in and out of rooms. I perused the table and my dog appeared again; I stole out the back door and followed her, again, but the guilt started to set in. The poet would be disappointed (she had even started texting me the verses of her poems). And of course there were the children. The children! I lost the dog.

Gurus and hippies wearing white sheets and grape leaves in their hair flooded the streets. In one building they were eating vegan meals upon tables and chairs they carved with their own hands. Colorful Tibetan flags hung from the rafters. I tasted the food, sour like cigar leaves, and spit it out. I called out the names of my children over the din of the crowd. I went frantic out into the street where a white wave came rushing toward me, and I feared being trampled. But they lifted me up into the air. I crowd-surfed then grabbed a-hold of the sacred flags against a building to hoist myself up. Someone reprimanded me. I said, "Fuck off, this situation is dire." I hoisted myself off the wave of the crowd. I knew I had it in me to rise up, so I ascended over the brambles, over a guru who followed my projectile from below.

When I landed, he gave me a smoking gourd, said if I spent time with it in my hands it would teach me how to use it. I ran through the dispersing crowd with the smoking gourd in my hands, calling the names of my children.

Mind, Mine

Wicked stealth cloud
pallid, consuming gloom
you speak doom

your sticky fingers
your wormy, hell-bent mouth
you whisper in my sacristy
while I lie supine

Mind, mine—this divine.

Here, a woman moves
the worlds above me
shakes her rattle about
my lumbering head

Take up the sword, she said.

And I lopped off your
handling hands, a toe, an ear

A wing sliced the air
and landed—one stern
sentinel hawk stare
with a design of eyes
upon his back,

We enter beneath him
into the Twilight Kingdom
of Beauty and Insight

And unexpected ease
where I do as I please.

Swinging shutters,
windows of air

Here my desk, there my lair,

I am untethered, winged
boundless
in pen, paper, and mind.

The Musee d'Unterlinden

Two American teenage boys point
to something wedged between a wall
and the Crucifixion.

A middle-aged French woman in a
chemise blanc and a jupe noir carries
an unraveled coat hanger. She maneuvers
the hook to snatch a petit oiseau. Drags
it across the ancient stone.

Le petit oiseau sits for a moment
in the woman's hand, stupefied.

The woman closes her hands over
the captured bird, carries it to an overgrown
shrub in the courtyard. Le petit oiseau
hops, falls, flies haphazardly to the
ground. Disappears.

C'est tous! The woman exclaims.

It lives, says one boy.
For now, says the other.

I am left alone with the absent bird.
Thinking of its fledgling's wings,
its fledgling life.
Of faith.

A Roundabout to Wilderness

I was on the phone and driving, something I did not like to do, but it was my dead friend talking now, and I didn't want to put her off. I had just run into her brother, my former lover, and I told her how we parted amicably. "It was fine. He's doing fine," I said, reassuring her, feeling again tentative about my driving and talking. The connection started to go bad, and I hung up immediately, having a good excuse now, and drove toward home free of distraction. But I circled back again to the same parking lot where I had met my ex. I tried the roundabout again and again came to the parking lot. On the third time around I stopped at a nursery and went inside to ask for directions.

The cement floor was wet from the melting of snow. There was a smell of wet earth, a display of broken shells and small figurines, ferns, people perusing relics. I asked the clerk for the way out, and she pointed to a side door. I went through and saw an opening torn in a chain link fence at the back of the parking lot. I went through. A wolf came and brushed up against me; his fur was fine, his eyes sharp. He loped away. A sheep came, a lamb, and she jumped into my arms. I put the lamb down, walked to a log cabin; inside was an English woman who told me she owned the refuge where the wolves and lambs run free. I came back out, observed the sloping downs, the outcropping of rocks, the deer gathered in the shade. I then exited through the same opening in the fence. Now here were a waterfall, a geyser, a country town. This was not my backyard. At the river's mouth, the firs loomed, hefty conifers that come with wilderness; it could have been Maine or the Bay of Fundy. I was definitely lost now, but the land, sacred, treacherous, called out to me, and I, stepping from stone to stone, heeded its call.

Winter Moths

Papyrus nymphs

    of no certain beauty

but certain lives

    not unlike my own

(in certain ways)

    color of dust, bothersome

like dust

    diminutive and diminishing—

an equilateral triangle

    of wings clinging

to the door, the window

    a visual staccato—iterations

in December

    welcome themselves in

crash into your face,

    spiral up, up, up

seeking

    what we all seek

in the end

    in the beginning

a portal, illumed.

Sojourn to Lucerne

I.

Logistics, maps abandoned. She
follows the river, sits
where the floodgates have opened.
Drinks wine.

At nightfall, the illuminated banks.
The fat troll at the bridge's gate lies
drunk and requires no fee. Above him
history resides in the rafters.
Death's debonair bones pose with the
fashionable flesh of life.

II.

She ascends above the ramparts, observes
the Earth's crook and curve, half-veiled.
Within the hour the last veil falls to
the soft tussle of bells.

She descends through a path in the wood
flanked by shrines and prostrates herself
at their footings. Murmurs
what she remembers of childhood
prayers.

III.

She scales the city's walls. Fingers
the holes in the fortress.

IV.

In the marble halls
she meets herself
the work of a dead master,
divine strokes of woman—her
own dark eyes, robust hips—
a kind of reckoning.

Dud

My grandmother's hands
were gnarled
like apple tree limbs.
Her nails, cut short,
painted pearly white for weddings.
Dud, my grandfather named her
in a letter from the war,
after bombs that don't go off.

(She answered to the name)

When I peel garlic,
my grandmother stands beside me
her dyed hair done up nice
an apron over her church clothes.
She directs the mechanics of my sauce,
the liberality of olio d'oliva,
while complaining about in-laws
and aberrations as reported
in the Daily News.

At night in her bi-level
made of cherry wood beams
and rooms decorated in Jesus and Mary
Moses sits on the sill, pure white.
If you lick him, he tastes like salt.

Downstairs Aunt Mickey and Uncle Freddy
smoke and drink highballs
while Uncle Rudy reads their horoscopes
in a filter of coffee grains.

My grandmother stops me on the stairs
next to the water from Lourdes.

Kiss God, she says, offering
the medallion of the Virgin and the Christ
from around her neck.

Kiss God.

The Shelf

You must feel the flow of God within you, I thought, as I ascended to the shelf again, elevated myself like a mystic high above the others. The brother of a friend had risen; they had all watched him do it. But he fell. He was plain-clothed now, mingling with the lay people below. I looked at the perched cardinals in their shimmering red frocks; they ascended before us, showed us it could be done. You see, I could stop a demon by just placing my hand on his malleable head and mold him. But sometimes it was a battle; the insidious being could fit just under my skin and it was too hard to distinguish whom to side with. The wrong thought would put me there, on the wrong side, and then I too would fall. Also, you couldn't just levitate in any room, only the one with the shelf. Get to the top of the shelf and you could see the stone angels standing guard at the river, and plastic flowers. And of course the roof joists.

I had known all the cardinals personally. The one with the white hair was the most compassionate; he had faith in me, despite my internal grappling. The last time I rose successfully to the shelf I nearly passed it and hit the ceiling. It was his face I was thinking of.

IV. Upon Waking

Doppelganger

I was the young maid in Girl with a Pearl Earring wearing a plain brown muslin dress and a blue sash over a white veil. I sat on the other side of the door in the pantry as one of the guests played the piano, his fingers trickling like water between a crevice and then pouring down, drenching everyone in sound. When it was over, there was a smattering of clapping, then silence, then an abrupt knock at the backdoor. It was the butler. He said that my lover had come to see me. Here? Now? I asked him. The butler touched his fine black hat and stepped back out into the night. I closed the door, went to the window and peered from behind the curtain. When I saw my lover, he was standing in front of his master's automobile reading the paper under the gaslight.

I returned to the table flushed; the other servants were still eating their dinner, suspecting nothing. My plate was there with its dash of potatoes and slice of beef. I had excused myself once to the confines of the pantry to take full advantage of the music on the other side of the wall, but now to leave entirely? I went back to the table unsure of what to do. Then, a second knock at the door. The window again; there were two people there now, a woman and part of a man. The way the woman's face looked in the glass—it could have been my lover's wife. I took a step back. The visitor knocked harder and one of the servants asked who was doing all that wretched knocking. I waved her away and opened the door. My father was there with the woman who resembled my lover's wife. The woman, without any hesitation, told me that this really wasn't my father; he was just someone who looked exactly like him, right down to the gold crowns in his teeth.

"It's not him," the woman repeated.

"This is a mistake!" I cried.

There was a scuffle at the table in the other room, the scrape of chairs. Outside one of the hounds was loose and hurled himself at the two visitors, knocking them down.

"You died!" I cried out.

"It's not him!" the woman yelled.

When the dog was properly retrieved, the two visitors—the woman who looked like my lover's wife and the man who looked like my dead father—crossed the threshold and passed through me.

"Doppelganger," I said aloud, feeling them tickle tendons and bones. "I'll call this one doppelganger."

The Path Through the Water

Deer legs, tail—white flash
Forest, running, running, arrow pierce
Blood, body fall.

Effervescence.

Early morning or Twilight
The moon is a cat's eye or a cradle
On the beach—fire. The sea parts,
Mounds of water on either side.
The path is clear.

Deer track, fox, bear. At this place,
Some Mecca, a burst. Light fills the water
While the natives dance. Some divine
Self sits on a throne, places the nameless
Sky on her head, a crown
Of air and light.

A bison lends a man his head
And hooves and the man
Runs free—a god.

Dark hollowed out log, humus, Earth.
The water parts to make room for us
We must go where we haven't been.

You don't trust yourself,
Says a being made solely of shattering snow.
It moves to the water
And the sea laps at its static edges.

We climb those mountains of water
Translucent now so we can see the life
Inside it—whale and calf, clown fish,
Coral, a web of iridescent beings.

We stand high, regard the parade
Of land animals walking the parted path,
Throngs of them gathering
At the fountain.

Time is not a river nor a sea.
It is staccato—
Here, there, here, there.

Here.

A hawk on the side of the highway
Peers down at me.
No snag of ego, no quagmire of thought.
You just live.

I long for that.

The Lost Dauphin

The children were already restless, and she, in her new dress with a curious stain on the collar, was slightly intimidated by having twenty children at her disposal and becoming all the more rowdy by the minute. Being a seasoned veteran of teaching, she knew she could pull something from the bag of tricks that comes with some fifteen years in the profession. She decided on the game of telephone, and she lined up the children—these children with mussed up hair, noses that always needed wiping—and handed the first child the message realizing then that of course the child couldn't read, so she whispered it into his ear, this ridiculously banal message (what should the message be, she panicked, just a minute before) and the child turned to the next and so on and so forth.

As the message passed from child to child, she went to close the door to the hallway, when suddenly her ex-boyfriend passed through the portal. X had, in one fell swoop, dismissed the children playing telephone, commenting something about her having her hands full, then passed through the exterior walls as smoke passes through a screen.

She tried her best to dismiss him as he did her, twenty years before, her heart beating against the impenetrable hardness of her ribs, white lights strung up on trees just outside her apartment, his hair pulled back to show his clean face, clear and certain.

But she couldn't dismiss him, not then, not now. Just the night before, X shared a bed with her and her husband, and she, eagerly, with heart brimming, opened herself to him and he entered her. It was her husband who watched from over her shoulder, pitying her, knowing her rampant desire to be loved and the heartache she was to feel by this heartless engagement. X withdrew prematurely, put on his clothes, packed up his things, and went back to the home he shared with his wife and kids.

So here he was now, casually walking through her life again, but she went about doing her job nonetheless, keeping the children in line, peering up at the clock—9:20—class would be soon dismissed for recess, and she could go back to picking up the pieces, the colored construction paper, the blocks, Legos, tidy up (she was always, always tidying up), recollect herself.

The message came down to the last child and she asked her to repeat it, and the black-eyed child said one word: dauphin. The sentence, the original banal message (whatever it was) was now condensed to this, and she asked the children what it meant and hands went up. After everyone had filed out the door and she was alone, she repeated it to herself—dauphin, dauphin— satisfied this mystery now had a name.

My Anima, My Doe

A queen doe

Graced me on the back lawn
After my twins were born

Bowed her great head
For a blessing in the rain.

I walked the city woods
Every morning to get out

To clear my head, look for her
In the soft, littered marsh.

Once I found her eating acorns on the trail.
We faced one another—each to each

With neither faith nor fang, we were kin
Sisters of that fur, this skin

The queen hesitated, and my dog
Moved between us—a breach.

I did not hear a horn
When she rose up,

Her hooves tapping at the hoods of cars
Landing on the snowy bank

On the other side of the river.
It was not I who killed her.

At night my daughter writhed
Possessed, in her bed.

(You wouldn't hurt them, my mother said)

In the morning, my neck split,
Pain to accompany dulled pain.

From the window, white pillows of snow—

Hushed cries, soiled diapers,
Pills in the drawer,

Domesticity claimed me
Because I could not claim myself.

I know this to be true:
She didn't have a herd.
She didn't have other bodies
To keep her warm
She had eaten all of the Scotch pines
Half way up.
She had eaten things she
Shouldn't eat.

The Vets pitched tents back in those woods, then.
I had found remnants—bottles, sleeping bags

Clothing, junk food. Nips. Would I find her
Hanging from a tree, skinned?

Are we not always beholden to hungry mouths?

One morning I held the
Idyllic white city in my palm

Its white spires above whiter snow.
Below—the fisher's killing grounds,

Littered with feathers, limbs, skulls, bones.
My dog had found a buried hide,

The brown of the hide—I knew.

I went alone at sunrise with a shovel
Scared the hawks away from the carcass

I hacked at the ice and pain ricocheted off my hands
I hacked at the ice and found

Not a hoof, but a paw.

In March, the river began to thaw.
I stood at the top of the icy trail

Debating my precarious descent
When I saw her

Bounding from ice floe to ice floe
As light as the air of eternity.

Your deer is dead, said a neighbor, in April.
Her body had been photographed.

Her body had been ravaged.

I asked the woman who collected the needles
From the banks for her whereabouts.

I picked daffodils for a nosegay.
We searched the north and east sides

Of Green Hill and found neither hide nor
Hoof, nor bone.

Late August and the undergrowth consumed
Every last thing.

Rumor had it a herd of deer swam to Misery Island
And back. People in kayaks saw them gliding through

The water like wraiths.

But here on the north side of Green Hill, a rustle
In the dead wood of the brambles,

Beyond the old growth trees,
Beyond the thatched grasses of the marsh

The white off her back
Looked nothing like surrender.

Heart Failure

There were important feminist texts to read, texts by ancient women in the time of a ruling mother. I had marked them for research and brought the books with me on my weekend away to an island where I was staying with some women at a friend's cottage. The cottage was a wise investment; my friend had good business sense and I was envious of her. It was decorated as one would see in a catalog with hardwood furniture painted white, colorful textiles, abstract art, acutely placed votives, and bouquets of flowers. We all commended her on her taste.

Upon entering the place, I had the distinct feeling I had been there sometime before with my mother. I asked my friend about the fence that abutted the road. Was it always there? It was. I opened the front door and the yard was marked with Puritan tombstones with small white flowers growing between them. In the backyard there was a queen size bed with a sapling canopy. Another fence separated the cottage from a larger house with a picture window. You could see the modern decor of the neighbors' kitchen and the state-of-the-art appliances. You could also glimpse the neighbors themselves who painted themselves metallic blue for something to do. I saw them moving around the kitchen, making a big batch of paella, their bald metallic blue heads gleaming.

I opted to sleep under the sapling canopy under the stars; I sought to be slightly distanced from the rest. While out there, I read my ancient feminist texts, the beam of a flashlight lighting up the words. I was worried I wouldn't fall asleep in a strange place, but I did. I awoke the next morning to a commotion down the street. The paramedics were trying to save a German shepherd from heart failure. The guy at the gas station where the dog worked as a watchdog said that they used the defibrillators on him. He was up and around now, but we were all worried about his heart. I didn't want to go near the dog: I was afraid of his suffering. A woman came then, to take him home. She wasn't his owner, but she knew her. She was compassionate, the way she stroked his fine fur and looked into his eyes, and I felt relieved that she had come to take care of him.

I went back to the cottage remembering my own dog, how I didn't leave enough food for her. That was just like me, not to think things through; I was always ill-prepared because a part of me was afraid to go. Being away from home always brought anxiety and that was the big secret I didn't share with anyone.

Granular Thoughts

The cool marsh grass come late August, the sun a coin
for a lover's pocket. Legs of a white bird,
the water, silent like glass.
In the distance, waves. We hear them fall and plunder.

Something is hushed in the private space of the dunes.
The sand absorbs what we give it.

It was the girl who made up her own lovers
and killed them too, when their stories got old.
She never trusted her own hair.
She spun this yarn, kept other girls suspended
until she could eat them.

It was the woman who willed herself to fall
into the shadow as it shook on the water,
the shallow warmth would welcome her body
the boat, some sail, the air

and all that it lifts.

Therapy Dog

It had stopped raining when we arrived. We had gotten a ride with a friend, and we went into the hospital with its concrete façade weeping. I was hesitant to go, but something impelled me forward: I had to face my fear, see how deviated from typical humanity people could actually be. We checked in at the front desk where a dowdy, corpulent woman had issued me a badge. She said we were free to go to any room we wanted. My dog panted heavily, anxious. She was a three-year-old black Lab and I had not run her that day due to the rain. So she had all her nervous energy.

We walked the halls, passing orderlies in blue, mostly men, who acknowledged our presence with a nod of the head. My dog had her nose to the ground, seeking some scent that could give her a clue as to why we were there. Suddenly a woman burst out of one of the rooms. She was taller than I, wore faded jeans and a gray zipper down sweatshirt. She appeared to be fairly normal, save the outgrowth of a small hand over her left eye. Josie immediately went for her, greeting her with a sashay of glee. The woman petted her kindly, then grabbed my hand, and started tugging me down the hall, whispering in my right ear wildly.

She said most of the time she could control the actions of that small hand, but there were days when it danced so exuberantly, she had to follow suit, as if she were in a trance.

Let it be known that I was utterly transfixed by this appendage, that, at this point it was giving me a small high five. The woman—her name was Connie—said most of the people here had these outgrowths. Most had hands, but some had feet, some hands and feet, and some nearly a whole figure. "Oh no," she said, "We aren't allowed out in public. It's true, you know: it's too much for people to bear. We understand that. Besides they're good to us here. They really are." The small hand seemed to affirm what she was saying by making the "OK" sign with its fingers. I tried not to look at the hand—I was trained not to look, but any training I had left me entirely unprepared for this. Connie asked about Josie. "Is she a therapy dog? We've seen a few around here. We all look forward to seeing them, you know," she said, still grasping my arm.

We arrived at the cafeteria and there were mutants everywhere. The acrid smell was overwhelming. Several of the inmates came up to Josie to stroke her fur with their real hands, while the other ones, the protrusions, waved in the air, trying to get my attention. Josie succumbed to their petting, wagged her tail, but sometimes she caught a glimpse of one of the appendages and she'd prop up her ears, almost in alarm. But their cooing and petting had seduced her into thinking everything was normal.

I must tell you that these people were of all different races—some White, others Black, or Asian. Some were even wearing turbans, which concealed whatever outgrowth they had. The orderlies prompted them to go and eat lunch, not to forget to eat. "We always forget to eat," Connie said. A young man dressed all in white came up to Josie and stood in front of her but did not pet her. Josie lunged at him, wagging her tail, imploring he lay his hands on her, but he kept to himself. His lips were large and purple, like two inflated inner tubes, and quite suddenly, he opened his mouth and a sound droned out, something like a foghorn, and with it, a growing bubble. The bubble grew larger as the sound grew louder. I recognized the sound; it was a deep om—the same sound Tibetan monks chant in their temples. The cafeteria became quiet, even my dog became calm. As the bubble filled the air in front of us, the deep om settled inside me, easing every nerve. I felt a welling up, like I wanted to sing. Then the man was silent. Connie let go of my arm. One of the orderlies pulled out a whistle and blew it to round up the inmates. Josie got spooked and started to bark. I pulled her leash closer, but she sideswiped me, and I was caught off balance, tumbling to the floor, while she bolted.

I ran through the halls calling her name with the inmates mimicking me until a myriad of Josies were echoing off the walls. I ducked into a room with the door open. An old woman sat in a chair with a rose petal quilt over her lap. She was not fazed by my intrusion and stared blankly ahead at the barred windows, as a small appendage, a head, was pushing through her white scalp, trying to be born. I saw the pink insides of its small mouth as it let out its first cry.

When I returned to the front door, the corpulent woman was gone, and something dark was huddling under her desk. I grabbed its leash, but just as we passed through the doors, I saw that what was on the end of it was not Josie, but a priest, his black suit darkening now in the falling rain. The doors flung open. Out came Josie and the orderlies; I grabbed her by the collar, and we stood there watching as they tackled the escapee, wrestling him back into the hospital as eyes flickered behind the barred windows, a hundred eyes, a thousand eyes, and the rain bore down.

A Gathering of Women

I sat in an easy chair reading a book in my friend's house while the friend was vacuuming upstairs preparing for guests. The youngest girl came down and said she couldn't sleep. She was in her flannel nightdress and carried a small doll that was becoming smaller by the second. The girl was fond of me; I had a sensibility she could relate to, and she wanted to be near it, so she curled up in my arms while I sat in the easy chair reading. I maneuvered myself so the girl was comfortable. I propped up her head with a pillow; I stroked her hair as if she were my own daughter. Upstairs the vacuum moved this way and that in a room I had never visited. Then it stopped. My friend descended the stairs in a fit of anxiety, anticipating the arrival of her guests. "You're still here," she said to me. The daughter squirmed in my arms. I wanted to be rid of her because my legs were going numb; I wanted my friend to fetch the child and take her away, which she did, but not before the girl turned into a cat.

It was night now and my friend's guests were soon to arrive. I wanted to leave; I had no interest in a soiree. But my friend insisted I stay and gave me the guilt trip about how I never attended any of her gatherings. I thought of the long ride home through the woods. It was such a dark ride; I opted to stay for a while not only to appease my friend, but to defer the encounter with the darkness.

One by one, the guests arrived. My friend carried their coats upstairs to the guest room. They gathered around the table with newspaper clippings in their hands. I joined them thinking it was a séance and the clippings were obituaries. If you are going to tinker with the dead, you must have a talisman against evil, I told them. I hadn't particularly noticed their sterling bracelets dangling off their tan, slender wrists, their bleached teeth. I asked them what they thought Satan's face looked like. How horrible would it be? How disfigured? The women around me whispered into each other's ears. "This is not what you think it is," one of them said. "We're not here to conjure the dead. We came here to collectively ask for these things. The items here—" and the woman showed me the clippings—cutouts from department store circulars that included smart phones, tablets, designer shoes, etc. "These are the items we want," the woman told me. I thought of Christ then, how they gambled for his clothes at the foot of his cross.

I excused myself and went to the bathroom to hide. When I opened the door, I found a basin full of leaves. My friend found me there, trying to pee like a bitch. "Why are you so—different?" she asked. "So—strange?" My friend became visibly upset and worked herself into such a state, crying and carrying on. "Why can't you fit in? We got together to discuss the things we wanted, but you had to ruin everything by bringing the devil into it." I tried to ignore her, focus on the peeing, but couldn't. Why is she talking to me, I wondered. Can't she see I want to be alone? I stumbled out of the bathroom, out the backdoor. I came upon a ladder and climbed away from my friend as she continued to reprimand me. The ladder teetered in the open air as I climbed up above the trees, still trying to conjure up the devil's face.

Horn of the Moon

The dead crow is in the cupboard.
The wolves wait just inside the woods.
When I went to see the forms behind their yellow eyes,
I saw my own dog amongst them.

In a café, I saw his terrifying face on the wall,
his jowls—the beast, on the wall— who,
high up on a hill, under a glazed moon,
tore the spine from a man's back.
Was he food? A martyr? An offering?

I knew a woman who wished to be eradicated.
In a dream, animals cornered her,
set upon her, tore her to pieces.
Some being wove her back together
with threads of light.

She shone upon the back of an old elephant
that visited a shrine, tusks, tunnels of bone,
sun-bleached white after death's gnawing.
Others came and gathered, what was passed between them
was shared equally: gather the enemies, gather them
in a circle,

Hold them there.

About the Author

Laurette Folk's fiction, essays, and poems have been published in *upstreet, Literary Mama, Boston Globe Magazine, Talking Writing, Narrative Northeast, So to Speak* among others. Her novel, A *Portal to Vibrancy*, was published by Big Table. Ms. Folk is a graduate of the Vermont College MFA in Writing program and editor of *The Compassion Anthology*.

www.ingramcontent.com/pod-product-compliance
Lightning Source LLC
LaVergne TN
LVHW041302080426
835510LV00009B/843